ADVANC

CW01020007

"Anna Prushinskaya is a fierce and lucid writer."
—**Emily Schultz**, author of *The Blondes*

"Anna Prushinskaya's *A Woman Is a Woman Until She Is a Mother* is a frank, courageous, and beautiful meditation on the strange alchemy of migrating from one identity to another."
—**Helen Phillips**, author of *Some Possible Solutions* and *The Beautiful Bureaucrat*

"Anna Prushinskaya's essays are maps, are mirrors, are the magical objects lost and found by every wayward traveler in a faraway/familiar land. Every woman's experience of motherhood is unique, and yet I traced my own footsteps on the paths this marvelous writer laid before me. A lovely book – the kind you find yourself pushing into friends' hands and bundling up into care packages."
—**Amber Sparks**, author of *The Unfinished World and Other Stories*

"'Motherhood is an encounter, a shadow in mirrors, a beast lying low in the grass in the field,' writes Anna Prushinskaya as she grapples with the strangeness of pregnancy and birth. Russian-born, she swoops across the frontiers of country and motherhood as she contemplates the nature of language, pain, compassion, and the power of a woman's story. Meditative, curious and intriguing, these essays help us consider whether 'the things that come with life are worth it.'"
—**Toni Nealie**, author of *Miles Between Me*

A WOMAN IS A WOMAN UNTIL SHE IS A MOTHER

ESSAYS

MG Press
http://midwestgothic.com/mgpress

Some essays originally appeared in the following publications:

"A Love Letter to Woody Plants" was first published by *Great Lakes
Review* as part of the Narrative Map Project.

"Uncertainty: A Woman Is a Woman Is a Woman, Until, Sometimes,
She is a Mother" was first published in *Chicago Literati*'s Feminist
issue.

"The Quantified Baby" was first published by *The Atlantic*.

"One Mother's Answers" was first published by *The EEEL*.

Portions of "Calling My Grandmothers, Calling the Frontier" were
published initially as "Calling My Grandmother: Why I Write Fiction"
in *The Millions*.

"Remembering and Forgetting: Before and After Motherhood" was
first published by *Midwestern Gothic*.

ISBN: 978-1-944850-06-7

Cover design © 2017 Lauren Crawford

Author photo © Jessie Meria

Back cover brushes © gorjuss.co.uk

A WOMAN IS A WOMAN UNTIL SHE IS A MOTHER

ESSAYS

ANNA PRUSHINSKAYA

To my family: Thank you.

CONTENTS

LOVE LETTER TO WOODY PLANTS

To the woman in the parking lot of the park, who has found me crushing leaves, smelling them, and looking at the willows: I am giddy because I have identified a poison sumac. It grows on the trail by the water. They happen in Southeastern Michigan, and here are some ways to tell: Shrub or small tree; leaflets compound, sessile, with scarlet midribs; drupes white, persisting in winter.

I have been learning the names of woody plants this fall thanks to a special course at the college in town, a historic course, and sometimes I am overwhelmed with the trees. The distinctions between oaks, the tips of their leaves sometimes bristled, their buds sometimes tomentose, their acorns brimmed with fringe, where they are and aren't on a hill. And the maples. "Something like Acer," the graduate instructor says of them, meaning something common, mundane, easy to define. Silver, red, sugar, and box elder, they do their own thing. Thankfully, the Hawthorns one cannot distinguish, by the species at least. They have a thorny, suckering habit. They are part of one another. It is true that they have thorns and haws.

The shrubs that creep and climb beneath, I had not noticed. The vines with their special lifestyle, a specialist explains. They adapt; survive in high winds; have structures. Sometimes, they smother, they get a bad rep. A man comes to talk about soil, its microbiome with elements that outnumber stars. He throws acorns at the students to get their attention. A student asks how we could count the stars; the man explains.

I drive to somewhere by Highland Township, and towards Detroit, and to the border with Ohio, to find the right plants. There are places in Ann Arbor I had not considered, the glacial features. The forest changes. A place that felt common, felt familiar, is not the same place. I've only visited the class for weeks, which is to say, I know not much at all. Still, that is all it takes to make the forest strange and lovely, a place to touch and explore.

Often the forest is a backdrop. Now, as I walk and scan the paths for bark patterns, and then the understory, the leaves on everything, the way they move with wind, I become the backdrop to the forest. By the end, my senses are exhausted, and I listen. It is the time of year when I can hear the acorns drop, a time of year I hadn't noticed until now. I am not particularly spiritual, but I quiet. I think: Once I was an addict. Maybe I still am.

In the Mary Karr memoir *Lit*, she conveys a familiar situation. When in traffic, inching bit by bit, we don't think of ourselves as it. Traffic is the other humans. Prickles, spines, thorns, I touch plants with all of them. (Some things are structural.) What else can we learn from the woods, at a time when we need to learn from something more than ever I think, too sincerely. I crush leaves, I rub at bud scales.

The saying that encapsulates advice for winter identification, after the leaves have dropped: "Trust the bud." My instinct is to walk away from the forest, the way it's changed me in weeks. My instinct is not to trust it. I am hoping instead to find a place where I can. The woods in town, perhaps.

Does it help to know this was written while I was pregnant?

BEING
PORTAL

That writing was sincere, its bud descriptions and all. I was worried about revealing fondness for woody plants. What a strange thing to worry about at 3 am, a time when I am awake now often, thinking in excited ways.

I am pregnant, that is. Seven months or so. I am at the point that I have heard about, the point at which, suddenly, one feels very pregnant. That is, it is the experience of some women I've spoken with that the process is not gradual, the realization of it, in the way that fetal development is. Of the things that one hears about while one is pregnant, few are applicable. When the exterminator at the office notes that I am small for how far along I am, for example, I don't put much stock in that. Or the banjo teacher, who explains his wife's epidural, when and how it went. Or the man who does tai chi, who asks about the date of the "splash landing." (His parents coined the term in the 60s, having watched the astronauts on TV.)

Now the baby's movements can be seen by anyone.

I can hide in very large sweaters. Sometimes, I choose to hide. During Alice Walker's talk, I wear a taut top and see him stretch. His hands might be behind his head, my stomach like a hammock. I can feel his top and his bottom at the same time, something I hadn't felt before. The point is the baby is a boy. I had no expectation of the baby's sex prior to the pregnancy, as far as I could tell, though now that the baby is a boy baby, I think about the implications.

Alice Walker speaks at Hill Auditorium, the large, historic, acoustically-excellent concert hall at the University of Michigan. (It was built to fit the whole student body as it was in 1913. Famously, a pin drop on the stage can be heard anywhere in the auditorium.)

While the details of the midterm elections do not matter, it is the day after them, and people are disappointed. Alice Walker stands behind a large, wooden lectern, which has also hosted Martin Luther King Jr., Hillary Clinton, etc. I have been trying to be a good citizen. I have been trying to be informed. I have been trying to do so especially since I could vote, which was in 2008, when I naturalized. My family arrived in the U.S. in 1998, and before that St. Petersburg and Moscow, the Russia of the falling apart, and before that, Uzbekistan, its cotton, and its Aral Sea.

Alice Walker says of the elections, to the disappointed college town crowd of three thousand, that elections do not matter much. One should think larger, think more imaginatively. About the world, about the Fukushima Daiichi nuclear plant disaster, the radiation still moving, and the environment, the way nature intends to crumble within the near future, she suggests. Why desecrate the ability to vote when that ability is sacred, Alice Walker asks, or something like it, in my understanding of her view. The things that people go through to get the right to vote. Do not waste the sacred vote on evil. This is contentious.

Alice Walker espouses womanism: the world as organized and run by mothers and women. The "man" is in the best place he could be, the middle, surrounded by, mothering, energy, female, energy, but the point is also that he likes it there, in this Alice Walker world. I think about my body. My belly surrounds something male with its physical barrier, which I think is why I listen carefully.

Also, there is a connection with Russian literature. After the talk, I read the biography of Alice Walker, in which she recalls a trip to the Soviet Union: "I was so ignorant of history and politics when I went to Moscow and was taken on a stroll across Red Square, I could not fathom for the longest time who the Russians were queuing up to view in Lenin's tomb." (He is still preserved. In 2016, the *New York Times* followed up with Lenin, reporting on the costs of keeping up the body, polling Russians on whether it was worth it.) And yet she had fallen in love with the literature, Yevtushenko and Akhmatova, Dostoevsky and Tolstoy. "I read all the Russian writers I could find...as if they were a delicious cake...They made me think that Russia must have something in the air that writers breathe from the time they are born." I think to myself, *Despair?*

What then to make of bringing a baby into the world when the best Alice Walker, the woman sufficiently hopeful to espouse womanism, could muster is hope for an apocalypse, in this, our lifetime? She seems certain that the apocalypse will be the nuclear flavor, and in the winter that follows, there will be re-building, a recovery over generations of motherism, of thinking bigger, of hope. *Hope*, Alice Walker says, *never to covet thy neighbor's house, because then not peace, but war. The house shelled for some purpose, the house no longer their house, but shards.* "Hope never / to say yes / to their misery."

When I became pregnant, I thought about this question vaguely, the question of whether, on balance, the things that come with life are worth it. Now I am irreversibly pregnant, and I still wonder about birthing into an often-and-for-many horrible world.

In her best Anne Lamott manner in *Operating Instructions*, a memoir about her son's first year of life which merges suddenly into a memoir about her best friend's death, Lamott describes a conversation with an HIV-positive friend who says of the situation: "[Lamott's son] was meant to be born into the world exactly as it is, into these exact circumstances, even if that meant not having a dad or an ozone layer, even if it included pets who would die and acne and seventh-grade dances and AIDS." A woman is an opening. A mother is a portal, I think. A mother is not a drug.

(It is interesting how we are shaped, that addiction can alter the conception of motherhood, if one is first an addict and later a mother. It is interesting to note that Alice Walker's daughter is estranged from her mother. She denounces the way that "feminism" has shaped Alice Walker's approach to motherhood, to life. It's a two-way street, mothers and children, is the point.)

"Monastics were so connected to the human suffering of that pain that they set their bodies on fire," says Kim Tran in a recent essay on four ways you might be appropriating Buddhist culture. I worry about appropriating, and often when I think about politics, I remember reading about Buddhist monks. Is the approach to be present, to be mindful, but then, when time arrives, still to set oneself on fire? There's always that. *Do you want the hit or the serenity?* Maybe some version of the monks get both. What is the analog of this relationship in motherhood?

"I left organized religion for the forest," Alice Walker says. She is not a Buddhist but an everything-ist. Of her daughter's public denunciations: "In the same way that meditating in a cave affects the world, holding a space around these situations where you're not in the fray is very good." Of her own mother: "Because of her creativity with her flower even my memories of poverty are seen through a screen of blooms."

CALLING MY GRANDMOTHERS, CALLING THE FRONTIER

In Julia Cameron's *The Artist's Way*, the New-Agey creativity manual, she suggests we go for a more "gentle" God concept, not the punishing God familiar to many, the one who doesn't appreciate free-wheeling creativity. Along similar lines, in her memoir *Lit*, Mary Karr resists the suggestion that prayer might be useful until her life gets so shitty, she can't resist it anymore. Everyone's always bugging her to pray, too.

I have been "praying," though I've never thought of myself as the praying type. The prayers are mostly "thank you" and "please" statements. They don't end with me, but with other people and the world. I try to incorporate enemies.

Labor is a frontier, I think, and I search for the means of crossing it. I find Nancy Bardacke's *Mindful Birthing* by Google-searching "birth" and "mindfulness." On contractions: Think instead about expansions that run through the body. Then, they disappear, forever. Think of the present moment; do not think about the things that may or may not happen.

Birth classes are suggested, for those with the means.

There was no such thing as birth classes in the former Soviet Union, where the women in my family gave birth. I am going to be the first to give birth in America, another reason it's frontier-like for me.

My grandmother took a trolley to the hospital when her contractions were three minutes apart. The hospital was four stops away. She got there, and she had the baby, my uncle, her first, in an hour and a half. She calls it *stremitelnie rod'i*, lightning labor. She tells me to do *to chto trebuet dusha*, which means roughly to do *what the soul demands*. Except "soul" in Russia carries an expanse and sadness and a golden field of grass with lightning storms rolling, wild images that "soul," in English, for me, does not.

My son is that soul, she says. He makes his desires known in mysterious ways. She calls what is happening inside of my body "perestroika." She'd been waiting for me to call, she says, and I had felt it, and I called. *When God is willing*, she says. She tells me to get fresh air, to go on walks.

The other grandmother doesn't share the details of her labor. She speaks in generalities. She asks what is happening inside of me. She is the one who carried twins who were stillborn. She was in Uzbekistan and it was 1960, which didn't help. She tells me to tell my son that he is family. She tells me about her two-hour walks in St. Petersburg, the streets, mostly, and the cold.

My grandmothers are abstractions; they are amulets. I secret them away to help me across the frontier. I imagine photos of them in a well-worn locket. The way you'd carry myths or symbols. They are power and woman, but they are also flesh and blood and errors.

I seek the same on the American side. Caroline Henderson is the paradigmatic frontierswoman of the Oklahoma drought, the Dust Bowl. Henderson began homesteading in 1907, and, as the legend goes, began her love affair with the "natural loveliness of the unspoiled earth" after nearly dying of diphtheria at the age of 7. (Note: Howard Zinn. In this case, one woman's frontier is another woman's homeland.)

"Wearing our shade hats, with our handkerchiefs tied over our faces and Vaseline in our nostrils, we have been trying to rescue our home from the accumulations of wind-blown dust which penetrates wherever air can go," Henderson wrote. Perhaps at the edge of our capacities, we find the space to come into our own. Labor is an edge, another frontier of our own making, of possibility. When we're done, we stay there, stay mothers. Or, we make the opposite choice; the terrain of not motherhood is a frontier. Each edge has its own maker.

The writer Carolyn Chute is another American amulet. She lives in rural Maine. Her debut novel, *The Beans of Egypt, Maine,* follows a family in poverty there. In an interview that dates back to that time, Chute's directness grabs me. She explains, "I had a mother, a father, two brothers, a lot of different cats at different times – some at the same time – dogs, rabbits." Motherhood, a relationship parallel to the relationship one has to rabbits. This simplifies things.

The frontier clarifies values, helps to describe life economically. The interviewer asks Chute about the romantic notion of "the starving artist image." How does poverty affect the work? Chute responds: "When you're scared to death about where your next meal's going to come from, you're not very creative. I don't know how they got the idea."

Not the frontier, but the perseverance, the ability to, from the varying economy of these women's living, to describe the reality of things. Chute's debut novel made her money. After that success, she was met by the same interviewer: "No doubt people imagine that because you've broken out of poverty that so shaped *The Beans*, you will necessarily become someone else." Says Chute, "People say, 'Obviously you've escaped the cycle.' No, I haven't. I'm not leaving my homeland. I'm not uprooting. I'm not denying my people. People talk about breaking the cycle and escaping and all this crap. Escaping what? Your family? Your roots? I can't figure that out – why they think anyone would want to escape that. How we have to leave our homeland and our people to have a good life?" Henderson stayed in Oklahoma. The grandmothers continue, now in Russia.

People are part families, part random things that catch attention, part forgetting and re-building from the ground up. My grandmother, the one who lost her twins, is a woman among photographs: when my sister and I are young, and then when we are getting older.

My grandmother lives in Russia now, but I grew up with my family in Uzbekistan. The Soviet Union fell apart in 1991 or so, when I was getting ready for first grade. I remember watching the tanks on television. My mother had made new clothes for my knock-off Barbie from scraps of my uniform apron. (In the Soviet Union, students wore uniforms to class. Brown dresses for girls, dark blue suits for boys.) She wove bows into my braids, and the parents watched outside the school on the first day of class. In the classroom, we learned etiquette. To stand up when the teacher comes in. How to raise hands, our arms parallel to the desks. I remember fidgeting. Maybe this memory is universal.

When we came to the U.S. in 1998, for me, seventh grade, the Red Wings won the Stanley Cup a month later. It was very exciting because there were many Russians on the team. The kids were mean. I lost my accent quickly. I didn't have much English when I came, though my father was focused on language learning.

I was taken to a special Sunday school in Uzbekistan. I remember putting together a project, cutting out pictures from magazines. The project was a family photo book. I cut out a woman and I wrote, "This is my sister" in English under the picture. I cut out a picture of a couple and I wrote, "Here are my parents." I cut out some happily graying older people and I wrote, "Here is my grandmother, my mother's mother. Here is my grandfather, my father's father." I cut out a picture of a boy in a baseball cap, though I do not have any brothers.

My family's roots are in Siberia and in a small town by St. Petersburg. These generations came to Uzbekistan, insofar as I understand it, for work and to escape famine and repression. I have a nebulous concept of genealogy.

Usually people learn more by asking. Asking is hard at times because of the language barrier. I was twelve when I came to America. Sometimes, I tell people that I was thirteen, because twelve tends toward childhood. I want credit for my Russian-ness, or at least for an immigrant identity. Thirteen seems the right threshold for credit.

Some think that from eleven to thirteen is a liminal space for language. People can be naturally, proficiently bilingual when they get their second language during this time. Get the second language before, and you tend to lose the native language. Get the second language after, and the native language shows dominance, at least in terms of sound, of accent. My writing is in English, I think in English, and maybe my son will know English alone.

But I have an emotional connection to words or expressions in Russian that I've never felt to words in English. My Russian language is a day-to-day language. It's the language in which I tell my grandmother that work is good and what I had for dinner, that I will call her again soon. I read Russian novels, but I don't use that language in conversation.

My grandmother now lives in St. Petersburg. When I remember my grandmother, a few things stand out. That she canned. That she made a joke about printing money, a joke about her line of work. I don't know exactly what she did in the Soviet Union, but my guess from the joke is that it was some kind of accounting. Her husband, my grandfather, died a decade ago, and he was a taxi driver. I remember that he took me on rides. I remember that he'd gotten mugged on the job.

The pictures on my grandmother's wall we haven't seen in years. We are still children in them, and this is her idea of us. Sometimes I send her new pictures from America. She has a picture of me and my husband, for example. We are raking leaves. I am wearing purple jeans, a jean jacket, and cat-eye glasses. What must she think of this, her granddaughter with a green lawn.

People say that today distance is easy. In America, families are often on opposite coasts. They check in online, fly to see one another over summers or holidays, they keep up. This is not my experience of long-distance family. When I was younger, I often thought that it was more like prison. Now that I am older and less prone to self-pity, I understand that the prison analogy doesn't hold. Among other things, the brutality is missing. Still, the condition is permanent. There'll never be a time when we're together as a family. Sometimes I think, why try. There is something false in connecting, to check in about what's happening without the dinner together to look forward to in a few months.

A fellow expat once said to me that people of our generation who have stayed in Russia don't think about the Soviet Union as intensely as we who have moved to America do. I think this difference has to do with our liminal space of language, our emotional core, which connects us to the fall, keeps us thinking about the place, keeps us building stories.

I set alarms to call my grandmother. I don't call her for weeks that add up to months, and when I finally call her, I tell her that I will call again next week. I don't call her next week. I think about calling her each time that I say I will call her. When I call her, I can hear the background noise of the street. She says regular things like that she misses me. She asks about her great-grandchild-in-progress.

I read something recently that described stealing

as a lack of faith. We steal when we don't have faith that the things we need will come. When I don't call, I think I am stealing time. I do not have faith that at the end of the conversation about the weather, there will be something that turns out to be love.

I've been thinking lately about the way, when you wake up in one place someone else is waking up somewhere else at the same time. Or maybe even if it is on the other side of the globe, where it is night time, it is still the same moment. I have noticed lately that my grandmother is an abstraction. I don't live with her in the same time, the same planet. But sometimes when I walk to work and the light is right through the leaves and the wind is slow and it seems like the universe is connected, and I think about what she is doing at the same time as I am walking to work, which is probably reading a newspaper or putting together the jigsaw puzzle or looking at the printed black and white photo of us that has been up for a decade, I acutely feel that we are in the same world. (It is kind of like a ghost. When you feel a presence in a house, and you don't believe in that kind of thing, but right then you believe it.)

On Saturday, we were making brandied cherries for a wedding. I was pitting the cherries with a fancy plastic pitter that had a splatter guard, and it was like a wormhole to that time in Uzbekistan when I was eight or nine and it was summertime. The market had just gotten fruits. My grandfather knocked on the watermelons to determine which ones were ripe. We pitted the cherries with something metal, a device that looked like a thumbscrew, something medieval, and the cherries splattered everywhere, on our arms and on our clothing and the floor, and my aunt was there too. The windows open for the summer on the three-season patio, and the Uzbek neighbors downstairs, the tensions that seemed quaint.

Birthing reminds me more than anything of the barrier. It was similar with the wedding. When I called my grandmother then, she told me that she couldn't have her wedding celebration because her brother, an athlete and motorcycle driver, was killed right before and everyone was mourning.

As I write this, I am having Braxton-Hicks contractions. They roll through frequently and often. A dull ache spreads. One couldn't miss the labor, it imposes. The frontier arrives, a field of Russian soul, as the case may be, the dust storm above Oklahoma, the poverty, in Maine.

OUR SPHINCTERS, OUR BIRTHS

"There is nothing more important than how we are born. We have forgotten this fact for far too long."
—Alice Walker, on Ina May Gaskin's *Guide to Childbirth*

How are women's stories told? Who hears these stories? What do these stories do?

The power of a woman's story is apparent in some labor and birth writing. Ina May Gaskin is a woman who might be familiar to you if you're interested in motherhood; she is the "mother" of all contemporary midwives. She wears her hair in braided buns and, to me, looks like Joni Mitchell, if Joni Mitchell had chosen a different profession. Her *Guide to Childbirth* covers many things. The theory of sphincters, for example, of which the cervix is one. They close shut in the industrialized, anxious, sometimes male-dominated settings of some Labor & Delivery units. Her approach to labor is that it's natural. It has its own inherent power. But women rarely know it, lately, anyhow. The book is largely birth stories meant to convey that power. That structure made me curious. Is there something special about "women's stories?" If yes, what makes them that way?

Sophia Kruz is a filmmaker. Her current project is *Little Stones*, a film that focuses on women who tap into the power of the arts in service of "women's" issues. For example, Kruz has traveled to the favelas of Brazil to film a graffiti artist who raises awareness about domestic violence, and to India to follow a choreographer who uses dance to work with victims of human trafficking. The project interested me in several ways. In terms of its content, *Little Stones* focuses on the stories of four women who themselves use various art forms and storytelling modes to mine and produce action in the realm of "women's" issues. And in terms of its process, Kruz has also had the unique experience of partnering with another woman to produce the film, working closely with the cinematographer Meena Singh.

This second bit was not without challenges. When Kruz first began work on the project, she knew she had wanted a woman cinematographer from the outset. She explains this through the context of stories: "We would be interviewing domestic violence survivors and sex trafficking survivors. These would be difficult conversations. Anything I could do to make the interview subjects more comfortable with telling their stories, I wanted to make sure that I did." Finding her collaborator Singh was difficult; the film industry is notoriously male-dominated, Krus says. Kruz reached beyond her usual network of contacts to find Singh, and the full significance of their partnership didn't strike her until they were both in Brazil.

Kruz says that she often didn't get to hear the stories until she sat down with her interviewees and started to talk to them through the interpreter. She interviewed another woman graffiti artist named Jupes, who spoke in Portuguese. "We just asked her to tell her story, and it turned out that the story needed very little translation," Kruz says. A domestic violence survivor, Jupes was tortured by an ex-boyfriend and had nearly died. "I realized how incredibly privileged we were to hear these stories and to be able to process them," Kruz says.

"Stories are used in public contexts to inform or educate, and this disproportionately affects women, and especially women of color," Colette Ngana tells me. She specializes in bioethics and begins with Henrietta Lacks, a woman whose story is well-known in the public health context. The cell lines from her cancerous tumor were used to conduct a significant body of research though she did not consent. Nor did she consent to the way that her story has evolved since her death. The author Carla Holloway, in her *Private Bodies, Public Texts*, quotes a scientist who describes the HcLa cells (as they have been nicknamed) as "one of the most storied biological entities of the 21st Century….HeLa continues to be used, exploited, and narrated." Lacks's family did not discover the research until years after Lacks's death; their discovery was coincidental. The way that the cells are described in some of these narratives, Holloway argues, "as 'vigorous,' 'aggressive,' and 'difficult to control'….incorporates some of the very stereotypes that black women of [Henrietta Lacks's] era struggled against."

Henrietta Lacks's story is an example of a woman's

story that's handled poorly, a contrast to the way Kruz and Singh strive to handle their subjects' stories: with consent. Ngana gives another example of such handling disparities in contemporary discourse: abortion. "Women's stories are used to stigmatize people who get abortions, but they are also used to combat stigma. We have protesters who put women's faces on posters, alongside pictures of fetuses, in very intimately vulnerable situations, used to shame." Then, there are the opposite scenarios in cases of abortion advocacy, when women share sometimes painful personal stories because they aim to help others.

The final example Ngana gives me is not specific to women, but it still resonates. In the context of end-of-life care, storytelling is a technique that helps families to make decisions and helps the medical staff understand what the patient might want. "*Would she want more extreme measures, would she want to be taken off life support, would she want to be tracheaed, would she want a feeding tube, would she want surgeries*...One of the best ways to ask these questions is to ask, *Who is the patient? Who is she?*" People tell stories. "They say, *She is a person who loves to read, loves to write, who is very active, who would go hiking every summer, who always said that by the time she was seventy she wanted to, I don't know, rent a villa in Italy and do X*." The process helps families understand that perhaps certain decisions don't align with how the patient might want to carry out her life. I can't help but think about disparities. Are women's end-of-life stories handled similarly to men's?

"Scholars take different views on this," Zarena Aslami tells me. Aslami is an Associate Professor of

Victorian Literature and Culture at Michigan State University and is also interested in the intersection of feminism and motherhood. I asked her whether her scholarly work has taught her anything about telling women's stories. "Someone like the French feminist Helene Cixous argued for *l'ecriture feminine*, a distinctively feminine mode of writing that men could actually produce as well. Some argue that some women writers pay attention to relationships, the domestic, the everyday, the private, the intimate in distinctive ways and in more detail than men writers do. But in my own work, I don't necessarily see the form or style of writing linked to the gender of the author in significant ways." She adds, "Your question is really provocative because it speaks to our sense that women do have different stories to tell, but also, obviously, different women, depending on their personal histories and locations across the social spectrum have very different stories to tell." I include this to say that to talk about "women's stories" is complicated and has its own history, and it is not one thing but a collection of theories as diverse as the stories they attempt to describe.

In this essay, I am telling you about Sophia and about Colette and about Zarina, three women's perspectives in service of an exploration, the exploration of this sense that I've gotten that birthing gives a "different" perspective, "different" story to tell, stories that have closed in on my own life as I navigate the public experience of pregnancy. The experience of pregnancy essentializes. A woman with the body of a pregnant woman tells her story often, and re-tells it, to the people who are close to her and to strangers. I do, anyway. But then, if she is me, on some days, she hides in very large sweaters.

What is the project of personal essay writing if not gathering stories in service of organizing thinking, in service of sharpening unruly, associative segments?

I am at the university library. The reading room is empty because the students have left because it is holiday time. The baby has the hiccups. He is firmly head-down and in place. I am so far along I should not travel, said the midwife. Once, I was in an abusive relationship, and I stayed too long. Many awful relationships, then the good ones, all folded into who I am.

Who is she? Who is the patient?

UNCERTAINTY: OR, A WOMAN IS A WOMAN, UNTIL SHE IS A MOTHER

I walked the dog twice. At times, she limped. An arctic chill has settled. In the film about Antarctica, a husband and wife are wintering at the large American base. They have the usual conversation about the weather, whether it is cold or not. Of course it is cold, it is Antarctica, the wife says. Typical temperatures range between -20 and -80. Yet the conversation persists. What the body can get used to, the husband concludes.

I walked five miles, all told. I am thirty-seven weeks pregnant, which is considered "late pre-term." A baby born after this point is normal. I wake up and think, maybe today I will give birth. I go on the long walks, and I think, *maybe this'll do it*.

I am feeling the feeling of precipice, of uncertainty. I am not a mother, but I am an "imminent mother-to-be" as a co-worker called it. I don't know anything about raising babies. I imagine calling my husband to tell him that the time is now. "The time" is only hours, or days, or weeks away. One month is not very likely.

Last night I thought: What this will be like soon, to not feel feet inside of me, to not feel hiccups. When I first got pregnant, I thought the opposite thing. How could I manage them, the months of movement, the sensation of something foreign from which one can't escape. I think about talking to the baby: *Before, when you were inside of me, you felt this way. Now, on the outside, you feel less so.*

It is a strange thing to know someone based only on what they feel like from the inside. You will only know one person in this way, I think. I hesitate to leave that sentence be. Before the pregnancy, I thought that I was certain that I wanted one child. Now, I cannot stop myself from hedging.

*   *   *

In *Mindful Birthing*, Nancy Bardacke calls for the "don't know" mind during pregnancy, a time when one especially wants answers, to know the when and the how and for how long. The truth is that one never knows, of course, is the point, but during liminal times such as pregnancy, this lesson is more obvious.

There are other times when the uncertainty makes me nauseous. "I'm ready!" I think, and "I am awake!" It is 5:48 in the evening, or perhaps the morning. I've just had tea, or I am getting ready to drink coffee. The anticipation is double-edged. Sometimes, it thrills, and other times it weakens. Adrienne Rich's *Of Woman Born* has arrived, a used copy, but I am too afraid to read it. I intended to go to a play tonight, but instead I am at home. I make plans to go to the art museum instead. I make plans to go to the planetarium. I make dinner appointments. As if the planning is a tether to the place where I understand who I am, the place that feels like it is slipping.

I woke up and thought: In America, to give birth, sometimes you need a birth plan. I woke up and thought: If you seek a pleasant peninsula, look about you. I woke up and thought: Is this baby moving? Is today the day I will give birth?

The night before, we met with the doula to go over the pressing things ahead of the labor. In early labor, alternate the active and the restful. In active labor, the main thing will be to go to the end of the rope and stay there. The end of the rope can come when one is interested in un-medicated labor, as I am. Our doula has a tool kit of skills, she says. She isn't one for giving false hope. We talk about good communication. We talk about where to park in case of snowstorms; our house sits at the bottom of the street and traps cars.

When she is at the door, we are in this uncertain place together, she equipped for it, while I am not. She will see me in a way that no one else will see me. We know this, but we have not done it.

*   *   *

After finishing the sentence, I took a shower. The shower was hot, and I worried about whether I was scalding the baby. I had taken many hot showers over the course of the pregnancy, the kind of thing that could have an effect, I thought to myself. I walked downstairs and chopped vegetables, beets and sweet potatoes, for roasting. My husband came home.

I felt a pop and a gush, the sort of thing that happens in the movies and is actually very uncommon. I spent my pregnancy pointing out instances of such unrealistic portrayals.

I didn't know at that point that my water had broken, that my son would be born six hours later, that he would come so fast and furious that he would be born in our house. That the EMS guys, whom my husband and the doula had asked to stay outside on our porch while our son was crowning, would ask me to spell my name and the address on the release form, after they'd come in to lend us a scalpel and blankets, to keep my son warm, to cut his cord. The spelling was for the release form, which was required because we didn't want to take a ride in the ambulance; we took our own car. No one else could spell for me because I was the patient. My son was on my chest, placenta still attached, blue and squirmy, and I remember that the EMS guy made a joke about my name, which is long but phonetic and of Russian heritage.

* * *

In her article "What happens to a woman's brain when she becomes a mother," *The Atlantic*'s Adrienne Lafrance argues that much of what happens neurologically during the initial days and weeks after baby is born is similar to what happens neurologically when we fall in love. The piece is interesting and logical, and I read it as I am awake and learning to breastfeed during the first night or two. My son wakes erratically, and he learns. What strikes me about the article is the image in its introduction. Lafrance quotes the artist Sarah Walker, who once told her that "becoming a mother is like discovering the existence of a strange new room in the house where you already live."

Our doula said that I may not feel anything for the

baby at first. That a labor that proceeds so quickly is shocking. The transition between pregnant and not pregnant, blurred. When the doula came to our house, she checked me. She felt the baby's head an inch from being born. I didn't believe it, and I believed it at the same time. The pain was full of pressure and burning, the way I'd read the pain should be at the end of labor, not at the beginning.

*　　*　　*

I remember repeating to myself a sentence from *Mindful Birthing*. The sentence is: "You and your baby are balanced on the edge of birth." When the baby crowned I felt that balance, and I felt the ridge. I hadn't known it then, but the ridge was the place where the plates on the top of his head bowed above his soft spot. I wanted to push him through quickly; maybe I didn't "want," I urged. When I look back at the labor, I regret that I did not stay in that liminal space longer. You and your baby are balanced on the edge of birth. The birth took over; it had its own energy.

I did not know the meaning of "shocking" then. I knew it when we returned to the house two days later. I sat down on the couch, the baby in my arms. I sat on the couch, the cheap grey one on which I had had my contractions, opposite the day bed, next to which I gave birth on the floor, and I began to cry. The house shifted. The rooms were the same rooms that had been in the house before. My sister had cleaned the floors and washed the towels. But the birth was in the walls and in the ceiling, and the floorboard stained invisibly, all referring to my son.

The article which quotes the artist Sarah Walker

was passed to me later in the morning the day that I gave birth. Said my friend who had sent the article around to the various moms and moms-to-be, "What is extra cool is that Anna on this list gave birth TO-DAY!"

The border between being pregnant and being no longer pregnant is more permeable than I had predicted. Before my son was born, I longed to be unpregnant, to have my body to myself.

Three days after a baby is born, when the milk comes in, women experience the largest hormonal shift in a lifetime, second only to the hormone shift that we experience at death. Our doula says this. The baby leaves a mark even when he is out of the body, is what she means to say, I think.

*   *   *

My mother comes as I am readying to leave the house for the first time, no baby. She tells stories about her birth experiences in the Soviet Union, the various things they had asked her to do with her babies. They took babies away from some of the mothers, for example, for days. She had counted my fingers and toes after I arrived because of Chernobyl, which had occurred around the time I was born.

I leave the house for the first time as a mother and I get coffee. I see a pregnant woman in the coffee shop. I realize that I no longer have the marker. Strangers won't ask me when I'm due. I am disappointed. The feeling is roughly that everyone should know what happened, that I just gave birth, this should be obvious from my body, the way that the pregnancy was. I want to tell the strangers: "I gave birth eight days ago!

I was pregnant very recently! He came early! He came fast and at home!"

On the street, three young women solicit donations for the children's hospital. We were just there, I want to say. We made a donation to the people who showed us how to install the car seat. We installed it very improperly when we rushed to the hospital after the birth. We carried it in with the base still attached. He was three weeks early, my son. We had to wing it with the car seat after he was born, accidentally in our house, and the floorboards in the living room were bloodied.

I note that the weather is moving, and I return to the house. It is to become warmer next week, when my son will be two weeks old. He is next to me bundled, his eyes open. He snorts, and the dog sniffs him through the mesh.

REMEMBERING AND FORGETTING: BEFORE AND AFTER MOTHERHOOD

Desires are already memories.
(Italo Calvino, *Invisible Cities*)

Minus twenty-nine days: I asked the universe to teach me something. I lost a glove.

Minus twenty days: Each day he is inside me is one day closer to the day he is outside of me.

Minus nine: It's a funny feeling, waking up each day with the thought: Today is the day I could give birth.

Five: I worry that giving birth will be like dropping acid. If you go on the trip in the wrong mindset, you're going to be fucked for the ride. My husband found a photo of me in which I look plump and tan and healthy, although that photo is from the Getting Fucked Up time of life. The night before the photo was taken, I smoked and drank and drugged. I am holding a baby in the photo. I vomited that day into the night.

Three: I have more "material," at least, which is how you think of birth and labor and becoming a mother, if you are a writer.

Two: The closer to birth, the more often the thought: What if I fucked up? There was wine and very hot showers. What you really want to do is birth a book, not a baby, my therapist had said in the beginning.

One (the day my water broke): Merry Russian Christmas.

Memories like aftershocks to an earthquake. There are three types of earthquakes, my mother says. Horizontal, vertical, and mixed. The mixed start one way and end another and level cities. Tashkent, where I was born, is on a fault line. In 1966, when my mother was toddling, much of the city was leveled. My grandmother was pregnant with my aunt. People slept outside for the rest of the summer, my mother remembers, which worked well for a city in the desert.

In a fairy tale, a woman is beheaded and forgotten. The soldier gets her dog with eyes like saucers, and another with eyes like windmills, and another with eyes like towers. He marries the local princess. I read the fairy tale to my son in Russian. My mother picks up the book from the bookshelf next day as I feed him. The book is from Tashkent, approved by its proletariat and printed the year that I was born. Its price was 1 ruble and 80 kopeks. A famous book, my mother says.

T-minus labor and labor. In my memory, the doula is beside the bed at the hospital as I am getting stitched. She describes the contraction she observed. I remember thinking at this moment of the pretty woman with the beehive and the cat eyes on the cover of the book *Birthing Without Fear*. She is catching her own baby, whose head at that very moment is emerging. *You and your baby are balanced on the edge of birth*. I remember hoping I would look somewhat like her during labor. This was before the catheter.

Two days after the labor, I put it down on paper. I was anxious about losing the memory. It rolled and wriggled in my brain. I gave birth to a boy at 12:55 in the morning. The car thermometer read 4 degrees. *These are the numbers.*

Things beginning with when.

When my water broke, we laughed and did not believe it.

When my mother called when we were on the way to the hospital. When they sent us home and told us to return if labor did not begin on its own. I was leaking and leaking.

When we picked up take-out, and the women who sold it to us saw our hospital stickers and asked if we'd just had a baby. We said, no, not yet, but we would have a baby soon. And they gave us brownies and ginger cookies, and one of the women said that she'd had a miscarriage at that hospital and that the nurses were wonderful. She had miscarried twins.

When we drove home. When the contractions became powerful.

When the doula said it was the baby's head. It felt soft and mossy. It was pyramidal. *You and the baby are balanced on the edge of birth.*

Whens that happened that I do not remember. Sometime in the hospital, my husband next to the baby who is under the heating lamp.

A friend says when he visits to meet the baby: You have that "Oh, shit, what have I done" look on your face. He says this "Oh, shit," stage happens and not to worry. He has two kids. He says: It'll feed into what you write and become.

Try, for example, to become aware of your heartbeat. The way the sleeve rubs against the wrist.

Three things I've read about babies at two months. They see more blue. They hear more echoes. Their brains have synthetic bundles, such that the walls may hum or wobble or taste of salt. When they stare at you, they do not mean it. It is just the older, reptile brain ceding control. Vision is in limbo, and its stumbles are similar to focusing on you, the parent, as you smile.

In a study, couples ask each other 36 progressively more intimate questions to discern whether they're a good match. Given the choice of anyone in the world, whom would you want as a dinner guest? What is your most treasured memory? How do you feel about your relationship with your mother? What, if anything, is too serious to be joked about? After the questions are through, the couple is prompted to look at one another for four minutes. With a baby, you skip the questions. There you are, staring, and an hour has passed. Hello, baby, it is mama. Where is mama? Mama is here. Sometimes, you are replaced by a window and often by a very dim lamp.

"Writing can give you what having a baby can give you: It can get you to start paying attention, can help you soften, can wake you up," says Anne Lamott. (*Bird by Bird* this time, a book about how to write.) The way I have written since the baby: between naps, between feedings, while standing and bouncing, while the fog of the night settles into the fog of the morning.

I return from the bar one night, one of the first nights out after the baby. Night means different things, and it is only 9 pm. A neighbor takes out the garbage. He stops to chat. Parenting is exponential, he says. What is amazing is that as a parent you have a particular window. You are the only person with respect to whom the child changes incrementally. You know when he flips, and that fifteen minutes prior he could not flip. You know when she says something, a sound she could not make before. You know when a thing happens and how to measure it, that it is unlike what it was. You have a window. You remember along the baby's timeline now, is the point, and not your own.

The neighbor read to his child in the evenings, the way one does. Board books, then picture books. One night, she asked what the things she'd pointed to were. She was pointing at the words. Sometimes, as a parent, one is called upon to explain language. Sometimes, as a parent, one is called upon to explain God. Tomatoes, monsters, the darkness underneath the bed or in the closet.

Our baby cried tonight. He is at the point when he wants to spend time with us instead of sleeping, because he is becoming more social, because he is beginning to smile. I add that to the stack of memories, try not to think about the next.

COMPASSION CHASMS

In her essay "The Pain Scale," Eula Biss explores the concept of pain through, among other things, the 1 to 10 scale that patients are presented with, which asks them to rank their experiences of pain.

How the scale maps onto actual life can be problematic. At the extremes, especially. Pain of "zero" seems impossible ("zero," in general, has this problem, though some complex mathematical problems cannot be solved without it). Ten, the "worst imaginable pain," relies quixotically on the imagination. As Biss notes, "Through a failure of my imagination, or of myself, I have discovered that the pain I am in is always the worst imaginable."

The scale, however, is useful. That is, it is better to have the scale than not to have the scale. To have fixed points, even problematic ones, against which to measure experience, the present to the past, the memory to the anticipation, is good.

In the case of motherhood, one is sometimes told that the "before" and the "after" will be different. A chasm opens. I was often told this would be the case with respect to compassion.

A scale does not describe the "before" and the "after" experience well. Perhaps the "before" and the "after" is more like what happens at an eye exam. Is this lens better of worse, a clinician asks and offers two choices in succession. The first sharpens, and the second blurs. Or, the second is too crisp, makes things vibrate and ache. Is this better or worse, more compassion or less? More selfishness? I have been self-assessing. When I do not mind caring for my son and I am exhausted, and when I do. When I hoard my time with him, and when I run away.

People describe the sensation of having a child, of being a parent, as similar to the sensation of having a heart that's out there in the world, walking outside the body.

Maybe you have come across the body scan in your brushes with "mindfulness" in popular culture. Sometimes this has also been described to me as practicing embodiment: the mind may leave the here and now, and the body never does. The body is an anchor to the present. During body scan, one brings attention to each part of the body progressively, noticing each part's own weight. When one is pregnant, sometimes this practice becomes a "being with baby" practice. The kicks and movements of the baby are counted as one's own bodily sensations, as the baby calls attention to him or herself from within, one can pay it attention.

After my son was born, I felt unmoored. I Google-searched my way to Jewel Heart, the local Tibetan Buddhist community center. I signed up for a course in "deepening awareness." I left the house for the first session in the winter dark after my son's bedtime. The feeling was of drifting and circling. There were three other people in the class, older men. We sat on cushions facing two teachers, each with red string around the wrist. Try not to think of your pain as "your" pain, the woman teacher said. Sit next to the pain instead, do not dive deeper.

During a contraction, one can practice body scan to go limp around the uterus. One can ask the body to relax around that muscle. I had tried to do this during labor. Now, I tried to do this around the muscles in my back, which ached with the crouching of breastfeeding.

What does this say about my capacity for compassion in the "before" and the "after?" The difference is that "before," thoughts of baby are OK, part of the meditation, body scan. After birth, the baby is distraction from the practice, of noting the body and its mundane aching. Is the thought of the placenta permitted, my former organ, now residing outside of me in the freezer downstairs? Some people make ravioli. Me, I am thinking of planting a tree above it in the spring.

I think about the baby anyway, the way in which he was a part of my body, grew from it. We are all a history of someone else's limbs. Is this why Alice Walker insists on "motherism" as the central guiding philosophy for the world?

When one is skin-to-skin with a baby, the membrane between humans, between one consciousness and another, is thin, seems permeable. The body of writing about motherhood, or feminism, is a body. As is the body of writing about pain and compassion.

Women who exemplify pain are sometimes saints and sometimes witches; they are sometimes as ordinary as a mother.

One mother, a friend, tells me about inflicting accidental pain onto her first child. This was when the friend first became a mother. She was very green. She clipped her newborn's nails in the dim light of the nursery. The skin broke, and her baby bled and bled. My friend taped a cloth diaper to her baby's finger, rocked herself and the baby to sleep. In the morning, the diaper was fully bloody. "You know how those diapers are," she says. They are thick and thready and absorbent. That is, they hold a lot of blood. Her daughter is older now and lovely and beautiful.

But then, there is also the childhood cancer, which affects in America roughly a classroom of children each month, says another friend, a mother whose child has become a warrior. When the news of childhood cancer arrives, the thoughts are not linear.

I think: And now for the most difficult pose of all, the triple espresso, the man with the Spanish accent who loves the fog says as he is leaving yoga the same time I am leaving yoga. The way the edge of the building where we met edges into the fog reminds me of Iceland, the cloud that ate us, as our son sat in the back and didn't know it. That was before this cancer. It is not our cancer. It is not the first. You say: worrying will not protect you. There is no money in poetry, but the money isn't what gets you from the man with the accent to the fear that you have of your child dying, so on paper, it has an edge.

We sit at a bridal shower, the mother who cut the finger of her baby, when she tells me this story about nail clipping. *There the young mothers sit*, the moth-er-in-law-to-be says of us during a toast about her fu-ture grandchildren.

One description of pain, birth, parenting: fero-cious moment-to-moment awareness. Another de-scription of parenting, not intended as that, perhaps: "in that blurred state between awake and asleep when too many intake valves are open to the soul...the skin of the soul is a miracle of mutual pressures." (Anne Carson) In Carson's *Autobiography of Red*, the son remembers his mother: "He would remember when he was past forty the dusty almost medieval smell of the screen itself as it / pressed its grid onto his face. She was behind him now *This would be hard for you if you were weak / but you're not weak*, she said and neatened his little red wings and pushed him out the door." Before becoming a mother, I thought of books as most-efficient compassion machines. Now I think that children are more.

One description of pain, birth, parenting: In-fancy lasts only weeks. Climb inside each moment and kick your way out. When I saw his heart beat, I was six weeks pregnant and in the emergency room. I had bled, and they weren't sure if he'd hold or if I would miscarry. The beat is not a beat but small vi-brations on a black-and-white screen. People say that the heartbeat changes everything for the woman; for me, things did not change then, but since birth, I have softened daily.

People attempt to measure compassion. In par-ticular in the clinical setting measuring compassion can mean measuring how the nurses and doctors are doing. There is a Compassion Measurement Tool

(CMT), for example, that anyone can try online. The CMT boasts that its focus is action and not feeling or attitude. That according to most up-to-date research, there is a "spectrum of compassion phenomena." Take the test to get your compassion score automatically. The basis is questions like, "In my practice of compassion, I experience the pain of the other person..." One can choose: Never, monthly, weekly, daily, and so on, to always. How does a mother answer? Can the answer include the child? When he cries, my milk drops. When other children cry, sometimes, too. The automatic compassion of the body.

"A recent gathering of compassion researchers reveals new discoveries about how and why humans help each other," writes Emiliana Simon-Thomas. Stephanie Brown, a speaker at this gathering, defines compassion as the motivation to help others. She does this *with all due respect* to other definitions. Compassion can be exhausting, is one view that she opposes. Compassion can bring fatigue, is another with which she disagrees. There is parenting, its absence of reciprocity, for example. Sometimes they risk death to help their helpless offspring. The trick is to recruit this mammalian system in other contexts, as when we help our co-workers or our enemies. Compassion has its roots in parenting, evolutionarily, anyway, she suggests.

Another study mentions "mindfulness" as a great tool for building compassion. Compassion, data suggest, comes more readily when people are aware of the present moment as it occurs, something more likely with mindfulness, the pain that the moment contains, sometimes belonging to others with whom we share that present moment.

A third study measures selfishness through asking its participants to assent to a set of statements. If a member of my family asks me to join him/her in his hobby or leisure-time activity, I will join him/her to make him happy, regardless of whether I like the activity or not. It is not terrible if I exploit others. Usually, I give in to the will of others. If the family budget is limited, I will give up my part. I sometimes act like a parent toward my parents.

I write all this and then the baby and I listen to Stevie Wonder. I cry and watch him mind the sun spots during "I Believe (When I Fall in Love)." It all seems so stock I want to omit it. I judge myself for wanting to omit this life from an imprint of life, this essay. Then, I judge myself for that, because I am a writer and I require honesty first and editing second. I am not compassionate, is the point, to myself. This is one example of many such compassion-less moments in my day, the very same day that I contemplate whether the baby's made me more compassionate.

I walk the dog who's been cooped up all day, and she growls at passers-by and animals. She lunges and jumps and twists. It is icy and she pulls and I pull back and I am angry. I do not empathize with her condition. We interview caregivers for the baby. One runs late because there is traffic on the highway. It is icy. I steam and imagine many lives for this candidate, unreliable lives, images for which I have no basis. I am not compassionate, is the point, to people and animals.

Maybe more compassionate for our own child, my husband says of my theory that our son has made us more compassionate. Maybe for children. No, I say, everyone, and I don't know why I'm sure given my own evidence to the contrary. "Children make you see distances," Anne Carson writes, the space between anger and something else. Maybe children provide for a new beginning, with their lives measured first in moments, then in days, then in weeks. Only after do we count in months and in years.

Probably the division between the "before" and the "after" is artificial. Every experience divides. Every thing can look different after something new. Motherhood doesn't necessarily alter one's capacity for compassion, or one's views on motherhood, I decide. The ants who have climbed somehow into the light fixtures look different moment-to-moment, too, no matter whether one's become a mother.

Sometimes my son wakes after his 3 or 4 am feeding and cries. I don't know for how long. I do not look at the clock. The truth is I am tired, and I am not selfless, and I want the bed and the pillow, and I think about the "before" the baby, this being who is new and relies on me, but who does not make me selfless. Perhaps that awareness is something, at least. After X minutes, I wake.

THE QUANTIFIED BABY

As someone who has worked with digital media, I often think about the ways that technology has made its way into our lives. This is the phrasing I prefer, the way technology has entered, as opposed to the ways in which we welcome it or incorporate it, because some of the ways in which technology enters into our lives are not consciously facilitated. Technology impinges, and only sometimes do we say "yes" or "no," or even think about "maybe."

During my pregnancy, the birth of my son, and the early months of parenthood, technology has been there to mediate every step of the way. I often wonder, as I spend time with my baby, my phone nearby, what the experience would be like without it. Though I strive to be mindful, rarely am I actively deciding to use the phone or not; I often pick it up as a reflex.

* * *

I suppose it all started with trying to get pregnant.

Though I had no reason to believe that I would have trouble getting pregnant, when it came time to try, I found myself Googling my way to various online "communities." Did you know that there are apps and forums for tracking basal body temperature? A BBT increase often indicates that ovulation has occurred, which is the optimal time to try to make a baby. On these forums, people share their temperatures, charts, qualitative descriptions of cervical mucus, so that all may benefit from the resulting database of knowledge. The month I got pregnant, I was diligently charting my own bodily symptoms on one such site. Waking up each morning, running to the bathroom to take my temperature and make the attendant observations, logging onto the site to record it all. My chart is now forever part of that structure of information. A woman might compare her chart to mine, hoping for a similar outcome—I got pregnant, after about five months of doing this.

Not only that, but there are also communities devoted to photos of pregnancy tests. I joined one such community. I peed on many sticks (In community shorthand, peeing on a stick is referred to as "POAS"). I joined this site because I wanted to "catch" my pregnancy as soon as it happened. My cycles were irregular, and I didn't want to miss it and keep drinking my daily glass of wine. Really I was peeing on all these sticks because I am neurotic, and this Internet community was perfect for letting my anxiety about pregnancy, birth, and becoming a mother run wild. It was great to see that I was not alone.

How this site works is one person posts a photo of a pregnancy test, and the other users on the site vote on whether it looks positive, negative, or not clear. Pregnancy test results seem like they should be obvious. But in fact, there is a window of time, before the concentration of the hormone human chorionic gonadotropin (hCG) surpasses a pregnancy test's sensitivity, when one can get the coveted second line, but that line is very faint. I couldn't ask my husband his opinion; he'd say, "Well, clearly that's negative," instead of staring at the strips like I did, looking for that ghost of a line. Other women on the site found their husbands similarly stoic. These women understood me. They used high-contrast and black-and-white filters (built into the site's interface) to get a better read of the tests.

I was in Northern Michigan without phone reception when I got my big fat positive ("BFP"), and so I never got the chance to get the epic "up" vote for it. I missed the chance to use the filters, the "inverse" filter with its ultramarine blue in place of the pink. I must admit, I was disappointed. I took a photo of the test anyway.

* * *

The popular pregnancy book *What to Expect When You're Expecting* has a corresponding app. The book famously compares the size of the growing fetus to various fruits (blueberry, orange, winter melon). With the app installed, I received instant weekly notifications at "new fruit" time, with an accompanying animated video of the fetus's development.

The best part was, again, the forums that were part of the app. One could join a group for women due around the same time ("January 2015 Babies"). These groups have thousands of members, in the U.S. and abroad, from the very young to what in medical terminology is known as "advanced maternal age." There were women for whom getting pregnant was easy or a surprise, and those for whom it was a difficult journey. Stay-at-home moms. Nurses. Women who miscarried.

In the first trimester, the posts were all about the chances of miscarriage, and the color of the bleeding. People bled bright red and lost their babies and posted their "goodbyes" to "January 2015." Then, it was about the genetic testing, which for most women is an option at the end of the first trimester. Women shared their bad results, and their false positives. Next, the sex of the baby, if they knew. Some people didn't want to find out and felt strongly about it. There was a "belly photos" thread, a workout support thread, threads dedicated to the successes and failures of husbands. Inflammatory conversations about abortion were unavoidable. In the final months, many people went into early labor. They shared lovely baby photos or horror stories; often the threads were updated in real time ("Going to the hospital now!" or "Getting the epidural!"). Many people responded with, "Am I the only one here who is still pregnant?" Never was anyone alone.

I also used an app called "Pregnancy and Mindfulness." I needed the mindfulness in part to manage my feelings about all the push notifications I got from the other apps I'd signed up for. This app sent them too. Reminders to breathe, not to forget my structured meditation practice, to check in with myself. How was I feeling at that very moment? "Relax," the app glowed purple, "and breathe." A big breathing audio effect could be heard if the phone wasn't muted. I liked the idea of that app, but I did not use it very frequently.

*   *   *

Once the baby arrived, I found a whole new slew of apps to be distracted by. One, called BabyConnect, lets caregivers track things like feedings, naps, and mood while parents are away, and that information synchs automatically with parents' emails and devices.

The level of detail is astonishing. The nap tracker is essentially a stopwatch. One hits "start" when the baby falls asleep and "stop" at the sound of the first awake cry. I suppose that's the intent, anyway, but for infants, the territory between sleep and wakefulness is vast.

With diapers, one also has options. Caregivers can choose between "poopy," "poopy and wet," "wet," and "dry." (Why change a dry diaper?) Add-on detail includes whether it's a diaper leak, an "open-air accident," which sounds like some kind of skydiving mishap, and a range of quantity from small to large. Should you need to note anything else, a free-range window for notes is also available. Feeding information can be similarly detailed. And there are options to track things like moods, types of play, etc. These things can be charted and graphed, and data can be exported into a spreadsheet.

I test the app so I know what it's like before asking a nanny or family babysitter to use it. My experience of the baby is mechanized. Always I feel like I am gathering data, observing, making decisions about how to properly record our interactions. He is starting to smile, and sometimes I miss the start of the smiles, find my way to them towards the end, because I am entering data. I won't need to enter the data forever, I suppose, the caregivers will. I could just read their reports.

I wonder whether the relationship between the caregiver and baby suffers with all of this data management in between. A computer keeps what's entered accurately; there are no cloudy memories about nap times or ounces of milk in bottles. There is less conversation between me and my son's caregivers at the end of the day, too. But the integrity of my relationship with him feels degraded by the measuring eye. That observation changes the observed isn't new, but I hadn't considered it in the context of watching my son. Do I want, at the end of the day, to stare at data, or to hear an imperfect but narrative human account of his day? Always there are options.

It's not all apps, of course. From the day he was born, I've been using my phone to time breastfeeding sessions. The lactation specialist was strict with me, 15 minutes, each side. Which means that I have often been browsing the Internet, checking and re-checking email, while breastfeeding, instead of staring at the fine hairs on the side of his head, instead of checking out the wax accumulating in his tiny ears, or the little flakes of skin between his eyebrows and near the corner of his eye.

When I have my phone nearby, I am also thinking about taking photos or videos, and texting and emailing them to my husband and family. Or posting them on various types of social media. I wonder whether what I send to his grandparents will be shared by them more broadly, and whether I mind or not.

*   *   *

There is plenty of talk and research about the importance of limiting screen time for babies and young children (Still, many adults I know let their infants and toddlers use their devices. Sometimes the kids even find new features the parents didn't know about.) But should new parents aim to limit their own screen time as well? Childhood has changed (as it has each generation), but parenting has too.

NPR challenged its listeners to track exactly how often they check their phones each day, and when the number proved to be unsurprisingly staggering (the checking-in adds up, on average, to almost three hours of phone time per day), challenged them to limit the number of times they check in "just because." Success was limited, too, at this challenge, for those who chose to take it on. The space that used to be the realm of "just being," and sometimes "boredom," was the same space from which creativity arose, NPR argued. The idea of the challenge was to encourage users to re-discover that space.

Consistency is good, but not always. Children have a lot to do with raising themselves. Write down what they say! An open heart is the primary factor. So reads a note card I received at my baby shower. I'd asked the mothers there for advice. This particular advice comes from my son's grandmother, my husband's mother. It begins to explain, I think, what I feel I'm whittling away when I'm staring at my phone while spending time with my son. Whether digital media can support the spirit of parenting, the card suggests depends on me, on how I let technology into my life.

When I am on my phone, and my email account

tells me it's updated "just now" as my son squirms and babbles and makes liquidy digestion sounds, I am pulled into something like the present moment, by him and by that phrasing, "just now." He is only two months old, and I do not know the answer to the question of exactly what I'm missing when I mediate our relationship with technology. It is just that I have a growing sense of *something* missing, something, perhaps, that springs from the place where nothingness should be.

AND
WORK

Before I became pregnant, I thought I would miss work and wish to return to it. I am still eager, in theory, but in practice, I can see that my understanding of this process was flawed. It is almost as if we are a unit, the baby and me. To say that I am gaining independence is strange, as one can't quite become independent from another part of oneself. That is, I did not understand that I would need to be independent from something that grew inside of me, though this may seem obvious.

I am sure that biology is to blame. Milk and hormones bind us, and when I create distance between us, the bond stretches thinner. Before I became a mother, I thought I would be eager to wean. I am still eager, in theory.

The transition from one type of thinking to the other, where I became the kind of woman I did not expect to be, was not abrupt but gradual. I wanted to escape the baby often after birth. I felt restless. Now, I want to climb into each second and expand it. The office approaches. I have been privileged to have special permissions that come with "I have a newborn" and "I recently gave birth" and "I am on leave."

A friend gave birth two days ago. Her photo from the hospital contains the same standard-issue blanket. The image floods me with that morning, the snow and the sunshine in the house before anyone knew he was alive. Before he had a name. Before I could miss the "before."

My husband is glad that the baby came early because we got him for three extra weeks. When I confront him about the idea, I say we would have gotten the three weeks anyway. He says had our son been born on time, our own allotments of life would not have automatically been longer. We only know what we have. The notion of our time together as discrete makes me shudder, because one is often only vaguely aware that the people who leave to go to work in the morning may not return home. Sometimes, that is, death can be sudden, is what I take away from that.

"Only then can we engage in mutual dialogue that does not reduce each of us to an instance of the abstraction called 'woman,'" ends an essay on feminism, which is in part about the writing of accounts of women's lives intended to be representative of such accounts. I do not know if mine is representative of anyone's. Do other women who have their own children have similarly strong bonds with them? Ours seems uniquely instantiated is the point, though of course I am aware that it is not.

Humor helps. "Don't stress about pumping at work. I mean, why would you stress about attaching a suction device to your nipples while you sit in a room

HR has assured you is 'private,' except for the absence of a lock on the door, while milk spurts into bottles attached to your engorged breasts, to the tune of Wee-WAH...Wee-WAH...Wee-WAH?" quips the blogger Pam Moore. I refer to my designated pumping place, a storage closet, as a milk dungeon, though my situation is better than most.

"There is a time for composing and a time for maternal thinking and, on happy days, time for both," writes the philosopher Sarah Rudrick. "Mothers, as individuals, engage in all sorts of activities, from farming to deep sea diving, from astrophysics to elephant training. Mothers as individuals are not defined by their work; they are lovers and friends; they watch baseball, ballet, or the soaps; they run marathons, play chess, organize church bazaars and rent strikes. Mothers are as diverse as any other group of humans and are equally shaped by the social milieu in which they work. In my terminology they are 'mothers' because and to the degree that they are committed to meeting the demands that define maternal work."

I am not an elephant trainer, though I did once aspire to be an astrophysicist. I do not organize or watch soaps. I have eaten a jar of peanuts, and I am a friend, and I am a lover, and my time that has been dedicated to learning to be a mother, though I would have learned had it not been dedicated, though I consider myself lucky to have had dedicated, paid leave time, because this is America and time with baby, especially time that is compensated is no guarantee, though and though, it is still difficult to think of it as transition, as a new beginning, as opposed to the end of something great. The office, that is. Work. Remember when you thought you'd want to run away from the baby?

When I left for work, he did cry, briefly. *He is not going to make this easy for you*, my mother-in-law told me. At work, I erected a wall between myself and my feelings. It is not that I do not feel those feelings, it is just that another person has them, a woman far away from me, not the woman in the storage room pumping with her breasts exposed to the office supplies. It is all very clean and vacuumed, thanks to wonderful coworkers who took it upon themselves to de-clutter.

In Icelandic fairy tales, for example, changelings and fairies and elves don't just take human shape. They also take the shape of animals; cows, for example, are common vessels, claims the collection I'm reading. Fairy cows figure prominently in stories, the morals of which sometimes have to do with marriage, and family, and motherhood.

One could wonder, for example, what he is doing at that very moment. Whether he is asleep or happy. One could adjust his wings and push him through the screen door, though the door is her own door, and she is the one who is leaving. One could paraphrase Anne Carson in veiled ways. She is a mother and a woman and she can only speak of herself in the third person at this moment in the storage room with the pumping and without the child.

I can build a milk bridge from the milk dungeon to the baby. I can and I can and I will.

THE OTHER FRONTIER: NOT MOTHERHOOD

When I come out from the storage room designated as my pumping area, sometimes my co-worker, a woman in her forties who does not have children, says to me, "How's it going, MOM!" The 'mom' part is emphasized, as it sometimes is also when I see acquaintances whom I haven't seen in a while but who have heard about the child. *Mom!* They say to me. When I refer to myself, I refer to myself as "mama" not as "mom," and I wonder if the etymology, in any case, has to do with "mammalian." My husband is a speech pathologist; he theorizes that the root of "mama" is the "m" sound, which babies' mouths make early on.

It is interesting to have "mom" as my primary defining characteristic because I do not think I aspired to be Mom. Women come to "mom" in many ways, and here are some: accidentally, aspirationally, matter-of-factly, with great difficulty. Having children is more matter-of-course than not having children is, by the numbers. The decision not to have a child requires justification, sometimes after public and unwelcome probing. Both of the women with whom I share my office do not to have children. One spent her life touring with artists, managing their needs. She rode on the backs of motorcycles in Italy to secure the right pizza for the dancers. I offered to document her adventures, the adventures she preferred to the having of a child, though she emphasizes also that she loves children and has nieces and nephews and is a proud aunt.

From my perspective, the choice not to have children is impressive because it indicates the sort of planning I did not engage in when I "decided" to have my child. I "decided" in that we agreed that trying seemed "fine," and that children sounded "good." I did not "decide" in that there was no long-range analysis in my case of what the child would mean, whether he was best for me, and for the world. This is the kind of thinking I imagine might be part of opting out, though it's hard for me to know.

In the book *Selfish, Shallow, and Self-Absorbed*, sixteen writers discuss their decision not to have children. The author Teddy Wayne, in his review of the book, mentions broadly the various reasons: personal, economic, environmental. Also, there are studies that indicate that for new parents, joy in life declines.

I meet Anne Carson's partner at work. I mention *The Autobiography of Red*, which I've fallen in love with in part because it resonates with my understanding of motherhood. *Oh*, he says. As far as he knows, it was not about that. The author needn't author the reader's imagination. Still, that the book is not about what it was for me, that which encapsulated in some way motherhood, is disappointing.

I learn that Anne Carson and her partner frequent

Iceland, and that in Iceland, so it goes, the children are not given names until they choose them. Sometimes a child is nameless for a year or two. The names are elected through behavior. When Icelanders get the groceries, they leave a gaggle of children in their strollers outside the store, another anecdote.

She didn't want to have a baby; she *wanted* to want to have the baby. This is how the author Jeanne Safer describes her choice not to have a child. She is one of the sixteen authors. It is funny to think about this careful, logical thinking in light of my current situation, standing next to the freezer and eating chocolate chips by the handful because I cannot stand to hear the baby cry. Did I choose this particular situation? Maybe vaguely, the way one chooses to find oneself in any mundane moment of life. An accumulation of tendencies and circumstances leads one to the freezer or the coffee maker, to a place one hasn't seen before, or to Iceland. I chose the baby, I suppose. I chose not to think about the choice too rigorously, which means something.

In her introduction to the book of essays by the sixteen writers who each chose not to have children, the author Megan Daum harkens to Anna Karenina. "People who want children are all alike. People who don't want children don't want them in their own ways." It is difficult to know how to feel about these sentences. Had I seen them before I was a mother, maybe I'd have agreed.

Another co-worker asks me if I am in a "love bubble" the day that I return to the office after my maternity leave. I say that maybe I am. I say that my feelings are many and complicated. I say that there is a lot of motherhood literature for a reason, on both sides of the issue, the motherhood side, and not. Some people find themselves in the situation of mothering. Choice is a range. For myself, I can say that my desire to have children is splintered. Had I known then what I know now, I still would.

The term "child-free" was coined by non-parents who chose not to have children. The term distinguishes these non-parents from the people who want to have children but cannot. Two very different animals, Meghan Daum notes, not in those exact words.

How to write about the experience of motherhood from this point of view, of recognizing its many animals? If in Iceland children choose their own names, is this the kind of choice like the choice to have children? *He has his own experiences all day long*, I think of my son, as he quiets and teethes, *and I do not know about them*. He does not choose, he encounters.

Motherhood is an encounter, a shadow in mirrors, a beast laying low in the grass in the field. I have stumbled upon it the way one might stumble upon a snake which is rattling which is not a tree branch which is against the bark in lightning. The carvings above and below it expand over years, allow bacteria through, allow for infection, make vulnerable. The succession of metaphors is imperfect. Morning is too many hours away, too few hours away, I think, as he falls asleep, and sometimes by choice.

Does it help to know that this was written after I became a mother?

ONE MOTHER'S ANSWERS

A WOMAN COMES ONTO THE STAGE WITH A BUNDLE. SHE SETS THE BUNDLE ON A TALL BAR STOOL IN SPOTLIGHT. SHE ADJUSTS THE BUNDLE. WALKS AWAY FROM IT, LOOKS BACK, WALKS AWAY. CLEARS THROAT. QUESTION HAS BEEN ASKED, AND THEN ANOTHER, AND THEN ANOTHER.

WOMAN

Answer: Virginia Woolf, probably. I don't question it, she is the first who comes to mind.

Answer: No. Well, maybe yes. But famous only amongst those I choose. Not broadly famous. Famous in a world of my choosing.

Answer: Do I rehearse what I am going to say in phone calls? A question about rehearsed answers must be answered more perfectly. Rehearsed, or short. No, I do not.

A perfect day is a day that includes impulse, is shocking to the mind, rewires. A day that is remembered as the day, not as a collection of days, or perhaps a Wednesday, or maybe sometime last fall. The day he was born, for example, or the day we were last together.

I sang to myself about him and was impressed. I do not usually sing. The song was mostly the chorus. He is a geniu-uh-us. Who is a geniu-uh-is? You are a geniu-uh-us. You are a geniu-uh-us. That's all? I was asked. And it was.

SHE SINGS THE REFRAIN A FEW TIMES. SHE SQUEEZES THE BUNDLE, SETS IT BACK DOWN ON THE STOOL. QUESTION IS ASKED.

WOMAN

Answer: I would choose the mind of a thirty-year-old, and then regret not choosing the body. Tracking backwards, the singing was two days ago. It was morning. The clouds looked mountainous, then their infrastructure melted, leaving only orange.

Answer: That's not local, is it. Bananas, neither.

Answer: I am very afraid of airplanes, but I do not think I'll die on them. When I think about death, I think about him. I have a hunch about the timing, but not the way. I have a hunch that I'll come first, and he'll go second. Maybe the hunch is a desire.

*SHE STANDS IN THE SPOTLIGHT WITH THE BUN-
DLE.*

WOMAN

We both love to have a conversation with light. We
both love fat rolls and raspberries. We both love goril-
las; the way they climb into beds and are rascals. We
laugh.

WOMAN LAUGHS AT BUNDLE SUGGESTIVELY.

WOMAN

I am grateful for the moment in life in which I am in-
scribed and which is during peacetime and for that we
have water and for that the world hasn't yet heated
to the brink, but most of all I am thankful for today.
When he was sick, his first fever, I held him, and he
talked and talked.

I wouldn't change the way that I was raised, but I
would change the location. Somewhere with swamps
or a river, so that I could boat and come of age like
boys do in the boy books.

Question: Take four minutes and tell you partner your
life story in as much detail as possible. Answer: His
eyes are saucers and he says nothing.

Question: If you could wake tomorrow having gained
one quality or ability, what would it be? Answer: Still,

he does not say.

If I had the crystal ball, I would learn sports and take bets. Everyone says that? Whether there is a reason to go on or not, truly.

I have dreamt of the banjo, and I did it while he grew, and now that he is out, I do not do it any longer.

Accomplishment? Answer: His eyes are saucers and he says nothing.

SHE PLACES ONE HAND ON THE BUNDLE, CA-RESSES THE LENGTH OF IT GENTLY.

WOMAN

In order: Honesty. My mother's eyeliner in the photo in which she is holding me and I am a baby (the way her eyes are similar to my own, but it is decades earlier and on another continent). Thirdly, that relationship, the one where cups were thrown and I was drunk and the knife was in the picture.

No.

I answered this in other ways.

Affection is a thrill. Love I manage if I have not had a day that's long with meetings, the first with him, which began at five a.m. I struggle to find love on a Monday, but sometimes on a Tuesday, or a Thursday. On the weekends, I am better. Sometimes I am overwhelmed with the ahead.

WOMAN CRACKS HER KNUCKLES, COUNTS THE VALLEYS BETWEEN THEM. THE BUNDLE HAS NOT MOVED.

WOMAN

The reddish tint of your hair, the way you've rubbed away a patch of it with your new movements. His eyes are saucers and he says nothing.

QUESTION.

My family, depends what you consider that. Warm, and warmer.

Answer: We are a two-way mirror, my mother and I. Me.

We are both in this room feeling X. His eyes are saucers and he says nothing. I wish I had someone with whom I could share X.

SHE MOVES CLOSER TO THE BUNDLE, MOVES BACK.

WOMAN

An embarrassing moment of life? Isn't that how we get from A to B? What it must be like not to have been embarrassed yet.

Your house, containing everything you own, catches fire. After saving your pets, you get the natural laundry detergent.

The death of my grandmothers because they are amulets. They contain myths and past lives and historic pools.

SOME QUESTIONS REMAIN.

Share a personal problem and ask your partner's advice on how he or she might handle it. Also, ask your partner to reflect back to you how you seem to be feeling about the problem you have chosen. How will I ever leave? How will I return to my life? His eyes are saucers and he says nothing. When he smiles, it is with one corner of the mouth but not the other. Mmm, he says. Hiss. Shh, I say. Finished.

BUNDLE DEFLATES. WOMAN MOVES CLOSER. SHE PICKS UP DEFLATED BUNDLE AND WALKS OFF STAGE AS LIGHTS DIM.

AFTERWORD

For my second son, who was born two years after this book was written, and who has made a different mother.

First of all, the first baby was not an orb.
What it feels like to push an orb with intention,
which is blue and bulging and alive,
is different from lighting,
"a little bit scary," as the first baby, who is not a baby,
who is a toddler, remembers each time the trees
are silhouetted against the sky
of the thunderstorm,
which was atypical, which was in January, which was
with snow.
"The trees are moving, they are a little bit wet."
But the trees are not moving, and there is no rain.
It is an unseasonably warm February day,
though a week ago,
when the second baby was readying for birth,
the weather was readying for snowfall.

Where are we anyway, this earth, this day the sixth
day alive
for some of us around here in this bed.
In Russia, "en caul" is called "born with shirt on,"
and it is still good luck. So you see,
there is hope for us in this universe,
when we can all agree on a symbol,
that which way life turns is shaped by the beginning,
that a baby is born, in fact.

ACKNOWLEDGMENTS

I read somewhere about interconnectess recently, that a good way to get at it is to think about ourselves as an intermediary between our parents and our children. This seems a good approach to books. This book wouldn't be around if it weren't for many people who supported the before and the after. But, let's be specific. Thank you to everyone at MG Press for careful stewarding of this project. Thank you to early readers of this book, in particular Juliet Escoria and Bianca Price-Wallace. Thank you to birth workers, and in particular the women who helped me with my babies, Sierra Hillebrand and Stacia Proefrock, because without those babies, this book wouldn't have been born either. Thank you to my close mamas and non-mamas who hold me up with their strength daily. Thank you again, as in the beginning, to my family. But the biggest thanks to Noah C., who's done all of the above and countless etc.

PHOTOGRAPHY

Anna Prushinskaya's writing has appeared in publications
like *The Sonora Review, The Atlantic, Pacific
Standard, Vol. 1 Brooklyn*, and others. She received
an MFA from Brooklyn College-CUNY, and she lives
with her family in Ann Arbor, Michigan. Motherhood
continues to shift and surprise her.